THE
MINDSET
of a
WINNER
GOD'S WAY

THE
MINDSET
of a
WINNER
GOD'S WAY

Discover God's Plan for You
Transform Challenges into Triumphs

REV. MARY JOHNSON

Paperback: 979-8-9904880-3-8
Hardback: 979-8-9904880-1-4

Printed in the United States of America

Unless otherwise indicated,
All Scripture quotations are taken from
The *King James Version of the Bible.*

Cover design and formatting: Lisa Monias at SouthRiverDesignTeam.com
Cover photo: Beerlogoff/Shutterstock

TABLE OF CONTENTS

The Mindset of a Winner

DO YOU KNOW THAT YOU ARE A WINNER? We were born to win! Each of us is designed like a well-oiled machine with the capacity to overcome every obstacle. This includes moving mountains of stagnation that keep us from going forward, tearing down mental strongholds, and defeating every enemy of our soul.

Our greatest enemy is not the devil, who was defeated at Calvary, or another human being, but the way we think: **"For as he thinketh in his heart, so is he…"** (Proverbs 23:7a)

The purpose of The Mindset of a Winner God's Way is about changing the way we think so that we will fulfill *God's original plan* for our lives. Our minds need to be transformed. The only way to change our lives is to change the way we think. The key to transformation is renewing the mind through the Word of God. **"...And be not conformed to this world: but be ye transformed by the renewing of your mind, that ye may prove what is that good, and acceptable, and perfect, will of God."** (Romans 12:2)

The Greek definition for the word **"renewing"** (ἀνακαίνισις) **anakainōsis:** *an-ak-ah' ee-no-sis;* often means *"renovation*: – renewing."[1] We have to apply *(repetition, intensity, reversal, etc.)*[2] while renewing our minds through the Word of God. Our life depends on it!

The Lord has given me ten mindsets for transformation. These are a set of principles meant to help jumpstart our thinking in the right direction. I do not give an exhaustive explanation of each mindset, but rather I give you an overview.

---

1 James Strong, Exhaustive Concordance of The Bible, Peabody, Massachusetts (1961), pg 11, 342
2 James Strong, Exhaustive Concordance of The Bible, Peabody, Massachusetts (1961), pg 10, 303

These mindsets changed the trajectory of my life.

I, the author, had developed some thinking patterns that were not in agreement with the Word of God. After applying these mindsets to my life, my thinking began to change, and I began to experience the power of God in my life. Negative thoughts that held me back began to drop off. I began to experience life in a new way.

You may have picked up this book because you know me and want to support me, and I appreciate your support. But more importantly, the winner in you will triumph as you apply these mindsets!

My thoughts and prayers are with you as you embark on this exciting and joyful, yet challenging journey!

Sincerely,
Rev. Mary Johnson, Author

A Winner Knows God's Make-up and His Own

GOD IS THE MOST LOVING, MOST KIND, MOST AMAZING, THE MOST MAGNIFICENT BEING IN ALL CREATION. He is Supreme over all creation. The most amazing truth of all is that we are created in His image!

Human beings are the only creation of God that is created in His image and after His likeness. God created male and female in His *OWN* image and after His likeness. There is no other creature created in the very image and likeness of God in all of Scripture. Not only are we created in His image, but He also created us, human beings, for His glory. **"To whom God would make known what is the riches of the glory of this mystery among the Gentiles; which is Christ in you, the hope of glory:"** (Colossians 1:27)

He has a perfect plan for every human being. God has not changed His mind or His original plan for you. He has the blueprint for your life, and it is a beautiful plan that is just for you!

Again, human beings are created to fulfill the plan of God for His glory. **"That ye would walk worthy of God, who hath called you unto his kingdom and glory."** (1 Thessalonians 2:12)

Understanding God's nature and my own has had the most significant impact on my life. Why? Because for so long I did not see myself the way God sees me. I believed in my experiences in life and what other people said about me more than what God said about me.

Once I began to understand my nature according to God and His Word for me, my life drastically started changing for the better. Now I have a different perspective on life. This is because the Holy Spirit has awakened my spirit to the truth of who I am in Christ.

Each human being was created in the image of God (Spirit) and became a living soul (mind, will, and emotions). Our bodies were formed from the dust of the ground, which is the lowest part of a human being's nature, and the body will return back to the dust after physical death. **"Then shall the dust return to the earth as it was: and the spirit shall return unto God who gave it."** (Ecclesiastes 12:7)

Mankind is made in the image of God. Let us therefore learn what the Holy Scriptures teach us about the nature of God and the nature of human beings.

God's Nature

"**G**od is a Spirit...**"** (John 4:24a)
Then we must know that God the Father, the Word, and the Holy Spirit are a Spirit also known as a Triune Being: **"For there are three that bear record in heaven, the Father, the Word, and the Holy Ghost: and these three are one."** (1 John 5:7)

Each Person of the Godhead has His own distinct role. We can see each of their roles in the beginning of creation. **"In the beginning God created the heaven and the earth. And the earth was without form, and void; and darkness was upon the face of the deep. And the Spirit of God moved upon the face of the waters. And God said, Let there be light: and there was light."** (Genesis 1:1-3)

When Scripture tells us that God created heaven and earth, this is God the Father leading in creation.

When the Spirit of God moved upon the face of the waters, that is the Holy Spirit taking part in creation. Jesus is the Word, so when God spoke, that is Jesus, the Word, taking part in creation. Even though the Father, Son and the Holy Spirit have three distinct roles, they operate as one and they work in harmony with one another.

Human Beings' Nature

HUMAN BEINGS ARE SPIRIT BEINGS; THE **SPIRIT OF GOD LIVES INSIDE OF US.** Which means we are anointed and full of God's power. Our identity and self-worth do not come from man but God. When we understand our nature, and who we are from God's perspective, we will never allow another human being to define us. Only God knows our true potential and what He has put inside of every human being.

You must realize that it's impossible for us (human beings) to understand our nature without understanding the nature of the Father, Son, and the Holy Spirit. Now, let's look at how human beings were created and the components that make up a human being.

According to (Genesis 1:26a) **"And God said, Let us make man in our image, after our likeness..."** I don't believe we hear this enough, so it's worth repeating human beings were created *in the image of God*. We established from Scripture that God is Spirit. The Father, Son, and the Holy Spirit are a Triune Being. A human being is also a triune being. A human being's nature consists also of three components, each component having its own distinct role.

The *first part* of a human being's nature is his spirit. A human being is a spirit that speaks! The spirit is the highest part of a human being's nature because it is the part that is created like God. Human beings are God's only creation created in His image and after His likeness, which makes human beings His Prize Possession!

The *second part* of a human being's nature is the soul. The soul comprises our mind, will, and emotions: **"And the Lord God formed man of the dust of the ground, and breathed into his nostrils the breath of life; and man became a living soul."** (Genesis 2:7)

God communicates to our born-again spirit. Our born-again spirit receives the information and communicates it to our soul. The soul is the part of the human being that determines how we think, feel, and make choices. Our soul will be influenced by the Spirit of God as long as our spirit remains connected to God.

The mind is the leader of the soul, so if we don't renew our minds with the Word of God, we will hinder the will of God in our lives. Why? Because the soul is not saved. In (James 1:21) it says, **"...receive with meekness the engrafted word, which is able to save your souls."**

A believer's soul is renewed by the word of God. Our renewed soul works in agreement with our born-again spirit. Most of the issues we experience in life are a result of an unrenewed soul. Do you see why it's so important to spend time with the Holy Spirit renewing our minds with the Word of God? It is the key to fulfilling God's perfect will for our lives on earth!

Satan is a spirit being. He also communicates to the spirit of a human being, but he has more control over a soul that has not been renewed by the Word of God. Satan speaks words to our spirit that agrees with his evil nature. He uses the spirit of fear, doubt, unbelief, rejection, etc., to torment the souls of human beings. Without the truth of God's Word in our hearts, we will believe Satan's lies and his words will manifest in our lives in a negative way. A renewed soul recognizes Satan lies and rejects them by the Truth and Power of God's Word!

The body is the *third part,* and it is the lowest part of our nature. The body is a shell, or oftentimes referred to as "the house." Nevertheless, God formed the body from the dust so that the spirit and soul will have a "house" in which to live. The body is the part of a human being's nature that receives its instruction from the soul and demonstrates the will of God on earth when it is piloted by a soul that has been renewed by the Word of God.

The Lord created every facet of our beings, but unfortunately, so many people look at the body as the real person; however, the body is not the real person of a human being. The real person of a human being is the spirit that lives inside the body. I know this may sound strange to many, but Satan has lied to humanity and tricked us into believing that the real person is the body. For example, in this country, let's talk about the color of a human being's skin. In this country, people have reduced human beings down to the color of their skin. The color of a human being's skin does not have anything to do with the real person living inside the body. Every human being is first a spirit, and the truth of the matter is you cannot see a spirit. Spirits are colorless, so human beings' real nature has no color.

The human spirit is invisible. The human spirit speaks to the soul, and then the soul expresses itself through the physical body. We have been taught wrong. The real person is your spirit, which lives inside the body! Remember, God formed the body from the (dust of the ground). So, it's just dirt! Your dirt might be lighter or darker than someone else's, but it's dirt! I pray that you receive this revelation.

The enemy wants to deceive us like he did Eve. He doesn't want us to know the truth, because we will no longer be an instrument that he can use to spread his hate to another race. In the mind of God, there is only one race: the human race. So many people are being mistreated, losing their lives, and have lost lives because of the color of their dirt.

What a tragedy for humanity and what an offense to God! If you only think God created the body to determine the worth of His creation, you do not know the wisdom and love of God!

God gave me a revelation about the color of a human being's skin. "He said the different colors of a human being's skin, represent His beauty." Human beings' skin colors are like a flower garden, and God is the gardener. Most flower gardens have more than one color of flower. Flowers are different colors, shapes, and sizes. For example, you have Tulips, Lilies, Roses, Daisies, Daffodils, and many other types of flowers. These flowers are all different colors, shapes, and sizes but it's the variety that makes them beautiful in a garden.

When God looks at human beings, and the various colors of our skin, the different shapes, and sizes of our bodies, in the sight of God, we look like one big bouquet of beautiful flowers. We are beautiful together, and beautiful individually, so in the sight of God's eyes, the color of your skin is beautiful!

The Holy Spirit revealed to me that the problem with racism in this country is a spiritual problem. One day as I was reading my Bible, I heard the Holy Spirit say to me "where do you see racism in the Bible?" The Holy Spirit was explicitly talking about the color of human beings' skin. As I pondered the question, I did not have an answer. He said to me, "The spirit of hate, which comes from Satan, is disguising himself through racism." Satan is using human beings to express his hate towards another race because of the color of their skin. Satan manipulates the minds of human beings to cooperate with his hateful spirit to execute his plans to destroy human beings.

It surprised me because I had never looked at it this way. The root cause of racism is hate. Because hate is the spirit of Satan, he must be dealt with by a force greater than himself and that force is love. God is love and love is more powerful than hate! God pours out His love in the hearts of those who believe in Him. **"... the love of God is shed abroad in our hearts by the Holy Ghost which is given unto us."** (Romans 5:5)

The Body of Christ is His representative on earth, and He has empowered us to take authority over the spirit of hate. Many people are not aware that the root cause of racism is hate, but the tragedy of that mindset is that hate towards other human beings is the same as hate towards God because human beings are created in His own image.

Adam's disobedience caused him and Eve to lose their God-given authority. Satan used the first man and woman, God's creation, after they sinned against God, to promote his evil agenda. As a result, Satan transferred his evil, hateful, and corrupt nature (spirit) to Adam and Eve. Satan then corrupted their minds with his evil, wicked thoughts, and imaginations. Adam's disobedience was the beginning of the fall of the entire human race. Every human being born after Adam and Eve was born in sin and separated from God.

Satan wants to destroy humans, and he doesn't care how he does it as long as it gets done! One of Satan's biggest tactics to destroy humans is racism. He has distorted the minds of people with his hateful thoughts to cause human beings to despise one another, especially because of the color of their skin. But for love to prevail in our lives, we must also get rid of the hatred (which is racism) out of our own hearts.

I know this is shocking to many of you, because you have never heard racism explained this way. To be honest with you, I have never heard it put this way either, but this is how the Holy Spirit explained the problem to me. The Holy Spirit is confronting racism, which is an evil, hateful spirit from Satan.

Another strategy Satan uses to destroy human beings is deception. God is exposing Satan's lies about the color of human beings' skin, which God sees as beautiful. He wants men and women from all walks of life to be free from racism. God wants us to be free to love and admire each other the way that He does.

God has a lot to say to those of us who have received Jesus in our hearts but hate their brothers or sisters in Christ because of the color of their skin. Here is what the Scriptures say about hating your brother or sister. **"He that saith he is in the light, and hateth his brother, is in darkness even until now. He that loveth his brother abideth in the light, and there is none occasion of stumbling in him. But he that hateth his brother is in darkness, and walketh in darkness, and knoweth not whither he goeth, because that darkness hath blinded his eyes."** (1 John 2:9-11)

This is a strong rebuke to those in the Body of Christ who say they love Jesus, but hate their brother or sister in Christ, or another human being. Remember, **"For the time is come that Judgment must begin**

at the house of God: and if it first begin at us, what shall the end be of them that obey not the gospel of God?" (1 Peter 4:17)

I pray that you receive your deliverance today in Jesus Name! Satan deceived humans by influencing human beings to despise the color of a person's skin. He knows the real person is our spirit. Until humanity understands the root cause of racism, which is a spirit of hate, Satan will continue to spread his lies to the next generation and the generations to come.

The Holy Spirit wants to correct this offense against God: looking down on people because of the color of their skin. The Holy Spirit also said to me "that some people will die and go to hell before they believe that they are not superior to people of another race." What a sad day this will be for those who make the decision to go to hell and spend eternity there because they can't be convinced that the spirit of hate (racism) is wrong!

Some people don't believe hell is real. Jesus Himself told the story of the rich man ruler who found out how real hell is when he died. **"And in hell he lift up his eyes, being in torments, and seeth Abraham afar**

off, and Lazarus in his bosom. And he cried and said, Father Abraham, have mercy on me, and send Lazarus, that he may dip the tip of his finger in water, and cool my tongue; for I am tormented in this flame." (Luke 16:23-24)

The rich man ruler was conscious of his state of being in hell because he was talking. Some people believe once you bury a person's body, the person is no longer alive. That is not true. The person is no longer alive and living on earth, but their spirit, which is the real person, is still alive. The person is in heaven or hell depending on whether they accepted or rejected Jesus Christ as their Lord and Savior.

Spirits don't die, which is why the rich man ruler was in hell crying out to be released from the torment which comes from the flames of fire!

God loves humans. We have a lot of work to do in this country and it starts with the Body of Christ, so as His representative on earth, let's show love to one another regardless of the color of our skin (our dirt). We have the Holy Spirit in us, and we know the real person is our spirit, and spirits don't have color. Again, I realize this information might be new for some, but

I know many of you will bear witness to the Truth of this in your spirit.

I challenge you today to renounce that spirit of hate and receive God's love in your heart, because Satan knows if you pass away without releasing the spirit of hate, you will end up in the lake of fire just like the rich man ruler, and Satan's final destination.

A Winner knows the Power of the Word of God

WE ARE LIVING IN PERILOUS TIMES IN OUR NATION AND AROUND THE WORLD. In the midst of turmoil, God's Word promises His people great peace. **"Great peace have they which love thy law: and nothing shall offend them."** (Psalm 119:165)

The key to peace is to love God's law like a friend. The Hebrew definition for the word **"love"** (אָהַב) **'âhab,** *aw-hab'; or* (אָהֵב) **'âhêb,** *aw-habe';* a prim. root; to *have* *affection* for (sexually or otherwise):–(be-) love (-d, ly, -r), like, friend."[3] So, when we love the law of God like a friend, we will have great peace. Jesus calls those who believe and obey Him, His friends. **"Ye are my friends, if ye do whatsoever I command you."** (John 15:14)

God called Abraham his friend. **"...Abraham believed God, and it was imputed unto him for righteousness: and he was called the Friend of God."** (James 2:23)

Our part is to believe in God and obey His Word, and we will be called the "friend of God." You might be thinking about your experiences in your life and believe it's impossible to experience God's Peace. But I want to remind you that the Scripture says in (Mark 10:27) **"...With men it is impossible, but not with God: for with God all things are possible."** If you are willing to be a student of the Word of God, receive His Words in your heart by faith, and apply them to your life, you will experience great peace through the power of God's Word. This power comes from the Spirit of God and His Word. His Word is true!

By God's grace, I am determined to experience His

---

3 James Strong, Exhaustive Concordance of The Bible, Peabody, Massachusetts (1961), pg 9, 157

peace in every area of my life. It's not enough to say we read the Scriptures but then don't apply them to our lives. If we do not apply them, they will not produce any fruit. The late Dr. Charles Stanley said it this way on his radio broadcast: "The Word of God does not become your own until you do it." Until we determine to love God's Word like a friend by obeying what He says, we will never experience His great peace in our lives!

Let's look at another example of the power of God's Word. There was a woman who suffered from a blood disorder for twelve years. This woman was determined to be healed. She heard that Jesus was in town, so she pressed her way through the crowd, so that she could get to Jesus. She came behind him and touched the hem of his garment: **"For she said within herself, If I may but touch his garment, I shall be whole."** (Matthew 9:21)

This woman envisioned herself healed and whole before she was physically healed. She reached out to touch Jesus, the Word, with a spirit of faith before she physically touched Him. She was speaking her faith as she was making her way towards Jesus. She knew within herself that once she touched the hem of Jesus' garment, she would be made whole. This woman made a demand on the power of God's Word by faith.

She touched Jesus with the Spirit of Faith, and Jesus felt the power released from within him the moment that she touched him. **"And Jesus, immediately knowing in himself that virtue had gone out of him, turned him about in the press, and said, 'Who touched my clothes?"** (Mark 5:30)

Jesus' disciples didn't understand why Jesus made a point of stating that somebody had touched Him, because He was surrounded by a crowd of people that was pressing on Him. But Jesus sensed that virtue had been released from within Himself, so He knew someone had touched Him in faith.

The woman's faith, which connected to the Word of God, and the power of God inside of Jesus was released and suddenly, the woman was made whole after twelve long years of suffering from her infirmity. I'm sure this was a day of jubilee for this woman, because she had spent all her money going to doctors, to no avail. Then God intervened miraculously through Jesus, the Word, and she was healed immediately!

Do you believe that the power of God's Word can heal your physical body from that sickness? Maybe you're not sick, but you are struggling with your finances. Do you believe that the power of God's Word can teach you how to get out of debt and stay out? God can give you a strategy for your finances that will eradicate all your debt overnight; He did it for the children of Israel, so He can do it for you!

In ancient Egypt, God instructed Moses to tell the Israelite women to borrow silver, gold, and clothing, so that the Israelites would not leave Egypt empty-handed. (Exodus 3:22)

The Israelites had worked thousands of hours uncompensated by the Egyptians. God knew that the Egyptians were going to follow the children of Israel to the Red Sea to try to bring them back into slavery. **"...Why have we done this, that we have let Israel go from serving us?"** (Exodus 14:5b)

God said to the children of Israel, **"...for the Egyptians whom ye have seen to day, ye shall see them again no more for ever."** (Exodus 14:13)

God spoke prophetically to the children of Israel what He was about to do to Pharaoh. God released the

waters upon the Egyptians and wiped-out Israel's cred-
itors forever! They were "indebted" to the Egyptians
until the Egyptians all drowned and the debt of the
Israelites was immediately canceled! The children of
Israel became wealthy overnight! That was God's strategy to get them out of debt, pay them for their hard
labor, and to make His people wealthy.

Don't limit God to what you see in your bank
account. He has ways to deal with your debt that you
have never thought about, ways that can change your
financial destiny forever! In (1 Corinthians 2:9) it says,
**"But as it is written, Eye hath not seen, nor ear heard,
neither have entered into the heart of man, the
things which God hath prepared for them that love
him."** Our responsibility is to meditate on the Word
of God and believe in Him. It doesn't matter what
situation you're facing right now: if you believe God
is able and you stand on His Word, you will see the
manifestation of His mighty ability and power!

So, what will you choose: God's promises or your
current circumstances? If you believe God's promises,
you will see the manifestation of the Power of His
Word just like the woman who had suffered from an

issue of blood for twelve years! And like the Israelites who were delivered from poverty and enslavement, *you too will be delivered, if you believe.*

A Winner Believes the Word of God

WHAT IS THE MIND? The mind is the dominant part of the soul which also includes emotions, will, intellect, and intuition. *The New Oxford American Dictionary* defines the **"mind"** as the element of a person that enables them to be aware of the world in their experiences, to think and to feel; the faculties of consciousness and thought.[4]

As believers, we must be aware of what God has given us in Christ. In (Romans 8:32) it says, **"He that**

---

4 Jewell, Elizabeth J. and Frank Abate. New Oxford American Dictionary. Third Edition, Edited by Angus Stevenson and Christine A. Lindberg. (Madison Avenue, New York, NY: Oxford University Press, 2010), 1112

spared not his own Son, but delivered him up for us all, how shall he not with him also freely give us all things?" Most of our experiences in life have been contrary to what God says in His Word belong to us, therefore it's urgent that we renew our minds so that we can experience the promises of God and live a fulfilled life in Christ!

A mindset is the established set of attitudes held by an individual. The word **"set"** means to be situated or fixed in a specified place or position.[5] So, our minds can be fixed or set in a position of limitation based on how we were raised, our culture, life experiences, relationships, etc. Maybe your mind is set at a barometer where you are unfulfilled and stuck. The Word of God says to set your mind on Him Who has unlimited possibilities for you and unveils talents, skills, and abilities that you never knew you had.

If you want to change your mindset, it will require real effort in studying the Word of God and you will need to apply pressure to reset your mind to conform to the Word of God. Why is this important?

5 Jewell, Elizabeth J. and Frank Abate. New Oxford American Dictionary. Third Edition, Edited by Angus Stevenson and Christine A. Lindberg. (Madison Avenue, New York, NY: Oxford University Press, 2010), 1597

Understanding the significance of renewing our minds is crucial for unlocking the fullness of God's promises in our lives. Many people are living below their abilities because of wrong mindsets. The Word of God holds the power to transform us into the image and likeness of God by renewing our minds. Without the renewal of the mind and the transforming power of the Word, we go around in circles repeating the same mistakes, never satisfied, and have no peace.

A winner is someone successful and victorious in life according to God's standards. His standards are far superior to those of the world system. The world follows a system which is contrary to the Kingdom of God. The world system teaches us to get a good education, a job, a big house, a fancy car and save a lot of money. There's absolutely nothing wrong with having these things, but it becomes a problem when we seek after these things more than seeking a relationship with God through Jesus Christ (Matthew 6:33).

The world system focuses on pleasing people through outward appearance, but the principles of the Kingdom of God are more concerned with the inward heart of a man. The world system entices us to have so many things, but without Christ, we will lack **"... love, joy, peace, longsuffering, gentleness, goodness, faith, Meekness, temperance..."** (Galatians 5:22-23)

The fruit of the Spirit comes from the Holy Spirit and by the Word of God. Through believing God's Word, we transcend limitations and obstacles as we grow and take on the mind of Christ. We must choose to believe in God and His Word. Jesus exhorted, **"... Be not afraid, only believe."** (Mark 5:36b)

When we believe in God, we will speak according to His Word. According to (2 Corinthians 4:13b). **"I believed, and therefore have I spoken; we also believe, and therefore speak;"** Doubt and unbelief also come by hearing and speaking words of doubt and unbelief. In (James 1:6b-7) it says **"...For he that wavereth is like a wave of the sea driven with the wind and tossed. For let not that man think that he shall receive anything of the Lord."**

Speaking words contrary to God's Word will negatively affect our belief system and ultimately our faith in God. Therefore, we must believe and speak the Word of God above our circumstances, hurt, pain, disappointments, and anything else that wants to compete with our faith in God's Word.

My faith in the Word of God led me to an unusual experience with God. I was living in my townhouse at that time and taught Bible Study to seventeen youths in my neighborhood. They all came to my house every Thursday at 7:00 p.m.

During this time, I received a vision of myself driving a minivan and taking young people on trips. This is something that I knew I would love doing. Because I believed what God had shown me in the spirit, I decided to go to the Nissan dealership and test drive a Nissan Quest minivan. Coincidentally, a few weeks later, I received a flier from my credit union about a used car sale event at Enterprise Rent-A-Car, so I decided to go.

At the used car sale, I saw a burgundy Nissan Quest minivan which was the same model I had test driven at the dealer. I liked the vehicle, but I knew it was over my budget. Then, the Peace of God came over me and the Holy Spirit spoke to my heart. He told me that I would not pay full term for the minivan, but that I would pay it off early. I told the salesperson that I was interested in buying the minivan.

The representatives from my credit union had already left for the day, so I had to come back the next day when the dealership opened and apply for a loan to purchase the minivan. The car salesperson told me that it was "first come first serve," and he couldn't promise me that the minivan would be there the next day. I believed in the vision God had shown me, so I didn't allow the words of the salesperson to discourage me. By faith, I confessed that the minivan was mine and that it would be there the next day. This was on a Friday evening. I then left and went to church.

On Saturday morning, I returned to Enterprise Rent-A-Car where they were selling cars, and the credit union was present on-site. I applied for the loan and immediately was approved. The loan officer finalized my paperwork and informed the Enterprise Rent-A-Car Sales Representative that I was ready to pick up my minivan. As I waited with expectation to take home my min-van, some confusion arose. The car salesperson began looking for the minivan and couldn't find it anywhere on the lot! He began running around, asking his colleagues if they had seen the minivan. The salesmen all began looking at each other perplexed.

Where was the minivan?

Finally, another salesperson walked over, and someone asked him if he had seen the minivan. I knew the minivan had to be there because I believed by faith what God had shown me, but I didn't know where it was. He replied that he had taken the minivan to the tire shop that evening to get new tires.

No, my minivan had *not* been purchased by someone else; rather, the minivan had been removed from the lot, protecting it from being purchased by someone else. Glory to God! Not only that but it had been equipped with new tires! The Lord had saved, protected, and blessed the minivan for me and for His use!

I walked away that day with the keys in my hand, as the owner of my burgundy Nissan Quest. I ended up paying the minivan off two years early just like the Holy Spirit had told me that I would. Hallelujah! God is faithful. He will do exactly what He says when we believe His Word and are in His will for our lives!

Whatever we believe in from God, we have the responsibility to do our part. God gave me the vision, but I had to act on the vision by going to the dealership: the minivan was not going to come to me. I had to continue to believe I was going to purchase a minivan and walk in that belief. I had to do my part so that God could fulfill His purpose for me and the youths to whom I was ministering. I did not know how this was going to happen, but *I believed God and His word to me* and stepped out in faith. As Scripture tells us, **"...faith without works is dead?"** (James 2:20b)

I challenge you today to confess, believe, and do the Word of God so that you too will develop the mindset of the winner that you are! Then you will walk in triumph!

A Winner Hears and Obeys the Voice of God

HEARING AND OBEYING THE VOICE OF GOD IS THE MOST IMPORTANT CHAPTER IN THIS BOOK. As believers, we need to know God's voice for ourselves, because there are so many voices in the world that are speaking. Many are contrary to the Voice of God. In reflecting on (1 Corinthians 14:10), which says **"There are, it may be, so many kinds of voices in the world, and none of them is without signification."** I have learned in my life that *the more time we spend with God, the better we will be able to hear His Voice.*

God has used some significant people in my life to speak prophetically about my life; eventually, I developed a hearing ear for how the Holy Spirit speaks to me. God uses people to speak into our lives to help us move to our next level. But beware: not everybody is sent from God to speak into your life. As (1 John 4:1) warns us, **"Beloved, believe not every spirit, but try the spirits whether they are of God: because many false prophets are gone out into the world."**

God uses prophetic voices to help guide His people. The Spirit of God in you will bear witness when a word is coming from God, and when it is NOT coming from God. Important: *anything that goes against the Holy Scriptures is NOT from God.*

I remember when I was learning how to hear the Voice of God. I was so eager to obey the Holy Spirit when He spoke to me. I would receive some instructions from the Holy Spirit and take off running. This was good and bad. It was good, because the Lord knew that if He told me to do something, and if I thought it was coming from Him, I was willing to obey. The bad thing was getting ahead of God's timing. I had to learn how to operate in God's wisdom and timing for my life. You can have an idea from God, but if you move ahead of His timing, what was supposed to be a blessing could become a disaster.

The story I am about to share with you is an example of getting ahead of God's timing. Several years ago, when I purchased my second home in 2006, I decided to rent my townhouse. I had heard a lot of horror stories about being a landlord. One night, I was sitting in my basement on the computer and the Holy Spirit spoke to me about getting a property manager. I immediately went on-line and started searching for a company that offered property management services. My eyes locked in on one company, so I called them the next day. I met with the property manager in-person. I was impressed with the company's services and the manager's professionalism and knowledge, so I signed up with his company.

At that time, my niece had just moved out of my townhouse. I was therefore looking for a new tenant. A friend of mine told me about a person she knew who was looking for a place to rent for her husband and grandmother. On paper this family did not qualify to live in my property. My property manager told me they didn't qualify. However, because they were believers and I wanted to help them, I decided to let them move into my house. Big mistake! God knew my heart was willing to help this family; however, the situation did not end well. I should have waited on the Lord to see if it was His will for me to let this family move into my townhouse.

Even though I had God's compassionate heart to help, I got my emotions involved. I should have allowed my property manager to do his job of protecting me and my property, because he was more than qualified to do it!

Oh, the story gets better. The family paid the first three months of rent, but then the late payments started. They lived in my house for several months without paying their rent, so I had to pay two mortgages. I started complaining about the situation to the Holy Spirit and He said to me that "He had sent me a property manager to protect me, but I had violated the property manager's judgment."

God knew this family was not His best choice for me. Because I got my emotions involved, there was a lesson I had to learn from this situation. It was a long, painful process to get this family out of my house. It taught me to listen more carefully to the Voice of God.

Once I realized what I had done, I repented before God and apologized to my property manager. Although God forgave me, He did not remove the consequences. I had to walk through that very difficult time by paying two mortgages until a new lease was signed. What was the lesson in this for me? It didn't matter that this family were believers.

I should have let my property manager do the job he was hired to do, which was to find me a tenant that was qualified to rent my townhouse. I ended up learning the hard way, and that was a lesson I'll never forget!

I have heard my pastor say many times that nothing is ever lost when we're in Christ. God used the experience to fine tune my hearing of His Voice. Although the Lord did not tell me directly not to let that family move into my home, I should not have overridden the judgment of the property manager to whom I had been led by God. This is how I got ahead of God's timing.

If you sense God is telling you to do something, make sure you pray and wait precisely for His direction and timing for your life. Maybe God is speaking to you now, but you don't want to do what He's telling you. You want to do it your own way.

In (Proverbs 14:12) it says, **"There is a way which seemeth right unto a man, but the end thereof are the ways of death."** In this situation that I spoke of about myself, I thought that I was doing a good deed by helping a family that was in need. Although my heart was to help this family, it was no excuse for me to not have prayed and waited on God's direction in this situation.

Maybe you are struggling because you are having challenges deciphering God's Voice from your own. We've all had those challenges of not knowing if it was God or our own voice talking. God will never tell you anything contrary to His written Word, so you can reject any of those voices that don't agree with the Word of God, including your own voice.

Developing your relationship with God is absolutely necessary for hearing His Voice. *Sit down with your Bible, read, pray, and commune with the Father, Son, and Holy Spirit. Take in the Word of God and listen for Holy Spirit's Voice to speak to your heart.* Remember that the Holy Spirit **NEVER** contradicts the Word of God.

In conclusion, today I know the importance of praying and waiting for God's direction and timing for my life. It took this encounter and others to sharpen my hearing so that I will always seek God's perfect will for my life. All decisions have consequences, so I hope my story will help you to *always pray and seek God's will for any decision that you make, so you will always be in His perfect will for your life!* No matter what decisions you face, trust in God's guidance, seek His will, and rest in His perfect timing.

A Winner Knows the Power of Confessing the Word of God

CONFESSING THE **WORD** OF **GOD** HELPS TO ALIGN OUR THOUGHTS TO THE **WILL** OF **GOD.** We must confess what God says in His Word and not what we see or feel. The Holy Spirit spoke to my heart several years ago and said to me "Satan is a master of the natural realm." Satan will always entice us to focus on the natural things that we can see, touch, taste, feel, and hear. This is the strategy Satan used to deceive Eve in the Garden of Eden. Satan is still using this strategy today to get us to focus on the lower things in life. **"For all that is in the world, the lust of the flesh, and the lust of the eyes, and the pride of life, is not of the Father, but is of the world."** (1 John 2:16)

Let's look at the scenario in Scripture of the three Hebrew boys who refused to agree to the demands of Nebuchadnezzar. He threatened them with destruction if the three Hebrew boys did not bow down to worship his god. Instead of heeding the words of Nebuchadnezzar, the three Hebrews boys believed God and confessed out loud what God said about their situation. There was a miraculous outcome because of believing and confessing God's Word.

Satan enticed Nebuchadnezzar to throw the three Hebrew boys, Hananiah, Mishael, and Azariah, into the burning fiery furnace because they would not bow down and worship his god. Even though Nebuchadnezzar threw the Hebrew boys in the fiery furnace, *they confessed that God was able to deliver them from the fiery furnace,* and He did! The Hebrew boys were facing death, but they did not confess words of doubt and unbelief, and because of their confession, they were delivered from the fiery furnace (Daniel 3:12-17). **"...for out of the abundance of the heart the mouth speaketh."** (Matthew 12:34b)

The faith that the Hebrew boys had in their hearts, they spoke it out and it came to pass. Whatever words are in our hearts, that's what we are going to speak. Let our words be words of faith!

Trials and tribulations will usually reveal what is in our heart. Nehemiah was another great example of confessing the Word of God in times of extreme pressure and persecution. Nehemiah was a servant of the King, and he heard that the wall of Jerusalem had been broken down and the gates burned with fire, so he wanted to help his people to rebuild the wall.

"And they said unto me, The remnant that are left of the captivity there in the province are in great affliction and reproach: the wall of Jerusalem also is broken down, and the gates thereof are burned with fire." (Nehemiah 1:3)

Nehemiah was saddened about the condition of Jerusalem, and the King noticed Nehemiah's sad countenance. The king asked him the reason for his sadness, so Nehemiah explained to the King his concerns for his people. Because Nehemiah found favor with the king, the king gave Nehemiah permission to go to Judah to rebuild the wall.

When Nehemiah's enemies heard that Nehemiah had led the Jewish people in rebuilding the wall, his enemies wanted to destroy him. **"But it came to pass, that when Sanballat heard that we built the wall, he was wroth, and took great indignation, and mocked the Jews."** (Nehemiah 4:1)

Brethren don't be surprised when your enemies rise and come from out of nowhere to try and stop you when you are doing the work of God! The intimidating threats against Nehemiah and the work of God sounded like this: **"And our adversaries said, They shall not know, neither see, till we come in the midst among them, and slay them, and cause the work to cease."** (Nehemiah 4:11)

Yet Nehemiah knew that God was with him. Nehemiah kept confessing God's Word and doing His work for the Glory of God. Nehemiah encouraged the Jews and their families by reminding them of what God had promised. **"And I looked, and rose up, and said unto the nobles, and to the rulers, and to the** rest of the people, Be not ye afraid of them: remember the Lord, which is great and terrible, and fight for your brethren, your sons, and your daughters, your wives and your houses. And it came to pass, when our enemies heard that it was known unto us, and God had brought their counsel to nought, that we returned all of us to the wall, every one unto his work.” (Nehemiah 4:14-15)

Let's continue to confess God's Word, do what He says, and leave the results up to Him. Most believers know that (Romans 10:9) is the foundational Scripture for salvation. It reads: **“That if thou shalt confess with thy mouth the Lord Jesus, and shalt believe in thine heart that God hath raised him from the dead, thou shalt be saved.”** This Scripture is not only talking about salvation for souls, but it is the foundation for how we receive the promises of God in our lives.

The Greek definition for the word **“saved”** is derived from safe; to save, i.e., (σώζω) **sōzō,** *sode'-zo*; from a prim. **(σώς) sōs** (contr. for obsol. (σάος) saŏs, *“safe”)*; to *save,* i.e. *deliver* or *protect* (lit. or fig.):–heal, preserve, save (self), do well, be (make) whole.[6]

6 James Strong, *Exhaustive Concordance of The Bible,* Peabody, Massachusetts (1961), pg 70, 4982

The word "save" is a complete health and wellness benefit package for the believer! Hallelujah!

Confessing the Word of God is a very powerful principle *but experiencing the manifestation of the power of our confessions is the reward!* I will talk more about the Winner knows the Power of walking by faith in the next chapter. God is only responsible for performing His Word, and we read about that in the lives of the Hebrew boys and Nehemiah.

Are you ready to believe God's Word and confess His Word as part of your daily routine? It is my prayer that you will daily confess what God says about you, believe it, and do it, so you too will see a performance of God's Word in your life!

MINDSET SIX

A Winner Walks By Faith

AWINNER KNOWS THE POWER OF WALKING BY FAITH. **"Now Faith is the substance of things hoped for, the evidence of things not seen."** (Hebrews 11:1)

God provides different strategies for His people to activate our faith. Whatever God tells us to do, we must do it! Even though the strategy challenges our faith, the provisions of a successful outcome of the strategy have already been made by God. We must activate the promises of God by faith during difficulties and hardship.

The strategies given to us by God can be different depending on the need. We will see this in the life of the widow woman, and in the story about the disciples and the two fishes and five loaves of bread, and how both situations challenged their faith. In each situation, they were challenged because they did not have enough, but the end results were miraculous!

Most of us have read about the widow women in (1 Kings 17). God instructed Elijah, the man of God, to go to Zarephath because God had commanded a widow woman to sustain him there. (1 Kings 17:9). Elijah had to leave from where he was because the brook had dried up. Some of you might feel like the brook has dried up in your life: but hold on! God has a plan for you! Let's see how God provided for Elijah and the widow woman.

Elijah saw the widow woman gathering sticks to prepare her last meal for her and her son. She believed they were going to eat their last meal and die! (1 Kings 17:12). **"And Elijah said unto her, Fear not; go and as thou hast said: but make me thereof a little cake first, and bring it unto me, and after make for thee and thy son."** (1 Kings 17:13)

God had a strategy to provide supernatural increase for the widow woman and her son. The key to the widow woman's miracle was in sowing her *first fruit* into Elijah's life by feeding him *first*. (Matthew 6:33) says it like this: **"But seek ye first the kingdom of God, and his righteousness; and all these things shall be added unto you."** Because Elijah was a man of God, when the widow gave to him, she was giving to God.

God was teaching the widow woman the way of the Kingdom. He taught her the importance of giving her first fruits into God's Kingdom. The widow woman obeyed the Word of God from Prophet Elijah, and what she thought was going to be her last meal was not her last meal. She and her son did eat many days thereafter just as Elijah had told her they would.

Now let's look at the strategy God used to challenge His disciples who had two fishes and five loaves of bread. In the Gospel of Matthew, there is a story of a multitude of people following Jesus and his disciples. It was getting late, and the disciples said **"...send the multitude away, that they may go to the villages, and buy themselves victuals."** (Matthew 14:15b)

The Holy Spirit revealed to me that it was the disciples' mindset of limitation as to why they wanted to send the multitudes away. The disciples began to reason amongst themselves about only having two fishes and five loaves of bread, which in their minds was not enough. Jesus responded by saying **"They need not to depart; give ye them to eat. And they say unto him, We have here but five loaves, and two fishes. He said, Bring them hither to me. And he commanded the multitude to sit down on the grass, and took the five loaves, and the two fishes, and looking up to heaven, he blessed, and brake, and gave the loaves to his disciples, and the disciples to the multitude."** (Matthew 14:16-19)

The Greek definition for the word **"blessed"** is derived from bless, praise; **(εὐλογέω) ĕulŏgĕō,** *yoo-log-eh'-o;* "to *speak well of,* i.e. (religiously) to *bless (thank or invoke a benediction upon, prosper):*–bless, praise.[7]

Jesus taught His disciples a principle of how to activate supernatural increase by faith, in the midst of lack. Jesus demonstrated this principle by *first* looking heavenward where all things are possible to them that believe. **"I will lift up mine eyes unto the hills,**

---

7 James Strong, Exhaustive Concordance of The Bible, Peabody, Massachusetts (1961), pg 33, 2127.

from whence cometh my help. My help cometh from the Lord, which made heaven and earth." (Psalm 121:1-2)

The *second* thing Jesus did was He blessed the two fishes and five loaves of bread. Jesus was teaching His disciples to bless the little they had by speaking well over it. I believe we will experience a demonstration of supernatural increase in our own lives as we apply this principle to our own situations.

Lastly, Jesus broke the bread. He said to His disciples, **"I am that bread of life. I am the living bread which came down from heaven: If any man eat of this bread, he shall live for ever: and the bread that I will give is my flesh, which I will give for the life of the world."** (John 6:48, 6:51)

Jesus was teaching His disciples that they had something to give to the multitudes. The disciples were not cognizant at that moment that they had Jesus, the very bread of life in the midst of them. Jesus is the Word of God and the bread of life, so the disciple could have at least imparted spiritual life into the lives of the multitudes by sharing the Word of life with them. The multitudes came for natural food to eat, but they needed the spiritual food too. **"...Man shall not live by bread alone, but by every word that proceedeth out of the mouth of God."** (Matthew 4:4)

As a result of this spiritual principle, the end results were miraculous! **"And they did all eat, and were filled: and they took up of the fragments that remained twelve baskets full. And they that had eaten were about five thousand men, beside women and children."** (Matthew 14:20-21)

The disciples wanted to send the multitudes away, but we must remember that we always have something to give to people. This shows us not to focus only on the natural things in our lives and miss the spiritual encounters with the Holy Spirit. Because Jesus is the bread of life, there are countless opportunities to share the Gospel of Jesus Christ with a dying world, so we should be sensitive to the Holy Spirit and allow Him to lead us.

Living by Faith is how the believer overcomes the enemy. In (1 John 5:4), it reads: **"For whatsoever is born of God overcometh the world: and this is the victory that overcometh the world, even our faith."** The "whatsoever" includes you and everything that

God has given to you. This includes your home, business, children, job, and so on. It includes everything that concerns you.

Make the decision today that you are going to walk by faith. You will be so glad that you did. **"For we walk by faith and not by sight:"** (2 Corinthians 5:7)

Finally, walking in love is essential to seeing the results of walking by faith, for it is **"...faith which worketh by love."** (Galatians 5:6b) We must maintain our love walk for our faith to be effective, operative, and active. We must walk in love to see the results of faith manifest in our lives.

.

MINDSET SEVEN

A Winner Knows the Power of Prayer

A **WINNER KNOWS THE POWER OF A STRONG PRAYER LIFE.** Do you have a prayer life? What is keeping you from praying? Most believers know that prayer is communing with God, and that it should be an essential part of one's relationship with the Father.

There are dimensions of prayer that our spirit goes through as we pray, but I will only mention a few of them here. They are praying the Word of God, the Prayer of Faith, and Praying in the Spirit.

Praying the Word of God is giving God back His

word. According to (Isaiah 55:11) says: **"So shall my word be that goeth forth out of my mouth: it shall not return unto me void, but it shall accomplish that which I please, and it shall prosper in the thing whereto I sent it."** As believers, we must speak and believe what God says in His word. He admonishes us to believe by what it says in (Mark 11:24), **"Therefore I say unto you, what things soever ye desire, when ye pray, believe that ye receive them, and ye shall have them."**

Whatever challenges you are having in your life, find God's promises in His Word, believe it, confess it, do it, and you will have what it says!

The prayer of faith can move mountains if you believe! **"...for verily I say unto you, If ye have faith as a grain of mustard seed, ye shall say unto this mountain, Remove hence to yonder place; and it shall remove; and nothing shall be impossible unto you."** (Matthew 17:20)

God has provided a way for believers to receive everything that we need through the prayer of faith. If you are sick in your body, the prayer of faith, which is the Word of God, will heal you from that sickness and disease if you believe! If you are a believer, you are spiritually healed. Your physical body might need healing, but you were spiritually healed the day you received Jesus in your heart. Healing was part of the atonement.

The prayer of faith is taking God at His Word; we must hide the Word in our hearts and water it by speaking it out loud over our situations. It will produce a harvest for us if we believe in His Word. **"And the prayer of faith shall save the sick, and the Lord shall raise him up; and if he hath committed sins, they shall be forgiven him."** (James 5:15)

I have experienced the healing power of the prayer of faith. Not long ago, I was lifting a ten gallon-glass bottle of water and putting it on the water dispenser in my house. I heard something snap in my body after I picked up the large and heavy bottle. I wasn't sure what had happened, so I went to the doctor and told him what had happened. He told me that I had torn my rotator cuff in my right arm. He gave me some exercises to do and told me if the exercises did not help that I would need surgery. The pain from the injury would come at night while I was lying down.

Although not severe, the pain bothered me some days more than others. I prayed and asked God to heal the pain in my arm. I was not in need of spiritual healing, but physical healing.

God had given me an assignment. The assignment required me to use both of my arms because the work was arduous. Oftentimes, we are not specific with our prayer requests to God. One day I was working, and I heard the Holy Spirit say to me, "You noticed you haven't had that pain anymore." I started moving my arm in ways that I could not have done before. God had miraculously healed my arm! I experienced the power of the Word of God in my body! Hallelujah!!!

Now, let's talk about another type of prayer. Praying in the Spirit is praying to God in our prayer language, which is an unknown tongue to man, but known to God. In (1 Corinthians 14:2), the scripture explains the meaning of speaking in tongues. **"For he that speaketh in an unknown tongue speaketh not unto men, but unto God: for no man understandeth him; howbeit in the spirit he speaketh mysteries."** Speaking in tongues is the evidence of being filled by the Holy Spirit.

There are some situations in life where our natural language cannot express how we feel or where human words are inadequate. Praying in the spirit (praying in tongues) allows our spirit to communicate with the Holy Spirit through groaning and utterances that only the Spirit of God can interpret. **"Likewise the Spirit also helpeth our infirmities: for we know not what we should pray for as we ought: but the Spirit itself maketh intercession for us with groanings which cannot be uttered."** (Romans 8:26)

Our voice is unique from any other voice. God wants to hear your voice, so pray! Prayer is so powerful! I'll never forget when I was in my room one day doing some housework. Suddenly, I felt an urgency in my spirit to pray. I started praying in the spirit, and the tongues were very aggressive. Little did I know the events that were about to unfold.

In less than an hour, my daughter called me and told me about an incident that had just happened at her friend's house. Her friend had graduated from high school and his family had invited his friends, including my daughter, to a cookout. During the cookout, some unwanted guests showed up unannounced to his house. The family did not know the young men, so they asked them to leave. These uninvited young men left, but they came back and started shooting at the young people at the cookout. My daughter was in the midst of this shootout! She was hiding behind a tree, her life in great danger! One of her friends saw her and called out her name and told her to run! She started running and her friend ran behind her, shielding her from harm. He was hit and shielded my only daughter from death. He took the bullet that would have hit my daughter and lost his own life. The young man demonstrated the love of Christ by giving up his own life and saving my daughter's life.

When I found out about what had happened, my heart broke for this young man and his family. I was overwhelmed with grief and gratitude at the same time. As a mom my heart ached for this mother who lost her son. I can only imagine her grief. Yet he had saved my daughter's life, and for that I am so grateful!

If I had not prayed, she might not be here today. I firmly believe that God used my intercession (praying in the spirit) to intervene and save my daughter's life. I was later able to go to this heroic young man's

Home-Going Service. The Lord used me there to encourage the young people in attendance to give their lives to Jesus during the altar call.

If I hadn't had a prayer life, I probably would not have heard the Holy Spirit when He prompted me to pray aggressively in the spirit!

Your prayers are so powerful they push back the forces of darkness! So, pray, because your life depends on it, or someone else's.

A Winner knows the Power of Fasting and Prayer

EARLY IN MY CHRISTIAN WALK WITH GOD, I WAS DEVOTED TO STUDYING THE WORD OF GOD. I developed a prayer life. However, I struggled to fast. That was not so easy.

Then God spoke to my heart and told me that fasting generates spiritual power. Jesus fasted and he said, **"Moreover When you fast…"** (Matthew 6:16a)

Jesus expects believers to fast. He is the best example of fasting and praying, and not yielding to the flesh.

"Then was Jesus led up of the Spirit into the wilderness to be tempted of the devil. And when he had fasted forty days and forty nights, he was afterward an hungred. And when the tempter came to him, he said, If thou be the Son of God, command that these stones be made bread." Jesus replied, **"...Man shall not live by bread alone, but by every word that proceedeth out of the mouth of God."** (Matthew 4:1-4)

The tempter is the devil, and he always comes to tempt us when our flesh is at its weakest. However, fasting strengthens the spirit man, so Jesus did not yield to the temptations of the flesh; He overcame His flesh by the power of the Holy Spirit.

Still, I struggled to fast, so I thought that I had a problem with food. The Holy Spirit told me that "I did not have a problem with food, but I had a problem with submission." I was stunned when God revealed that to me about myself, because I always try to obey God when He speaks to me.

He went on to explain to me why He had said this to me. The Holy Spirit said that when "He prompts me to fast and I submit, I obey and don't eat any food.

Likewise, the opposite is also true: when I don't submit, I eat food when I am supposed to be fasting!" This was so true. The wisdom of God will always defy the wisdom of man. I had never looked at it this way, but it was true!

I wanted to please God, so I began to undertake the discipline of fasting. I started reading different material on how to fast. I started small, by missing breakfast and praying during that time. Then I would continue with my normal routine of eating lunch and dinner.

I got comfortable with that approach, so I started fasting from 6:00 a.m. to 3:00 p.m. or from 6:00 a.m. to 6:00 p.m.

There were times that I needed an answer from God about an issue, so I fasted three days without food. God is so Faithful. He always came through for me and answered my prayers. I began to discipline my flesh and practice this powerful principle of fasting, and my prayer life went to new dimensions in the Spirit.

Fasting teaches us how to discipline our flesh by teaching us to yield to the Spirit of God and not to the cravings and appetites of the flesh. Most believers struggle to fast like I did, because they either don't understand the principle of fasting or they are not ready to lay down the flesh and give up their favorite foods and pleasures for God. However, we need to lay down such things by fasting and praying so that we can have divine encounters with God.[8]

Several times our church has undertaken a forty-day fast. During one fast, I had an encounter with Holy Spirit. I was in my bedroom in front of a window sitting on my lounge sofa reading my Bible. I would periodically look out the window pondering the goodness of God in my life.

The Holy Spirit showed me a vision of a garden. I said to the Holy Spirit if you want me to create a garden, you will have to show me how to do it. The first thing that He told me to do was to clean the land. He instructed me through the entire process and today I have a fully functional garden with all sorts of organic foods *without any chemicals* for me, my family, and friends!

During times of fasting and prayer, the Holy Spirit opens our spiritual eyes to see things in spirit realm that we would not otherwise see. During this time of

---

8 Please consult your physician before you undertake fasting.

consecration to the Father, the Holy Spirit reveals the Will of God to us. Fasting and prayer are important weapons that position the believer to have supernatural experiences with the Holy Spirit.

Obeying God during times of fasting and prayer is so important. As I said, the Spirit of God had laid on the pastor's heart to instruct the church to go on a forty-day fast. The Holy Spirit knew He was going to reveal to me the Father's heart during this fast. I have grown to a place in my life where I understand and know the power that is released through fasting and prayer.

If I had not acted on the vision of having an organic garden, this idea would still be in the spirit realm and not a reality. The unseen realm is more real than the seen, and we must become more comfortable in that realm.

Fasting and prayer weakens the flesh but strengthens the spirit: so that man's fleshly desires do not interfere with what God wants to communicate to us by His Spirit. As sons and daughters of the Highest God, we must remember the unseen realm, is the realm where all things are possible.

There came a time when I told the Holy Spirit that

I wanted to go to a new level in the Spirit with Him, a level I've never reached before in my spiritual walk. Our Church was still on the forty-day Daniel fast, so I decided to fast for fifteen days from 6:00 a.m. to 6:00 p.m. without food from within the Daniel fast. (I drank enough water.) I wanted to put more pressure on my flesh. Although I didn't reach my goal that time, I did manage to fast twelve days without food within the Daniel fast.

I believe the Holy Spirit honored my efforts. After I completed the twelve days, the Holy Spirit revealed to me why I didn't want to go on long periods of fasting. He reminded me of a bad experience I had and lost a lot of weight, and the enemy was using that experience to keep me from fasting for long periods.

I know that may sound strange, but that was my story. The Holy Spirit told me that it was a stronghold and that the stronghold had been demolished by the power of God! Hallelujah! I am delivered and free to fast as often and for as long as the Holy Spirit guides me.

Fasting is done in secret between you and God, so I personally don't announce when I'm on a fast unless it's a corporate fast. Otherwise, it's between me and

God. As a reminder in (Matthew 6:6), what we do in secret, He rewards us openly.

According to the Lord Jesus, there are some demonic spirits which will not leave our lives without fasting and praying. There is a story in the book of (Matthew 17:15-18), about a lunatic spirit that was tormenting a child. Jesus' disciples questioned Him as to why they couldn't cast out this spirit. Jesus answered them and said **"...Because of your unbelief:"** (Matthew 17:20a) The Scripture further explains in (Matthew 17:18), **"And Jesus rebuked the devil; and he departed out of him: and the child was cured from that very hour."** Jesus then said to his disciples, **"Howbeit this kind goeth not out but by prayer and fasting."** (Matthew 17:21)

So, if your mind is being tormented by the spirit of unbelief, it's surely time to turn down the plate and too fast and pray!!!

A Winner knows the Power of the Blood of Jesus

THE BLOOD OF JESUS IS SO POWERFUL IT ATONED FOR THE SINS OF MANKIND. **"And almost all things are by the law purged with blood; and without shedding of blood is no remission."** (Hebrews 9:22)

Yes, the Blood of Jesus is *exceedingly powerful!* It is *only the Blood of Jesus* that is qualified to satisfy divine justice. Because of this fact, Jesus redeemed fallen, sinful humanity with His own Blood and made a new and living way for us to return to God. **"But Christ being come an high priest of good things to come, by a greater and more perfect tabernacle, not made with hands, that is to say, not of this building; Neither by the blood of goats and calves, but by his own blood he entered in once into the holy place, having obtained eternal redemption for us."** (Hebrews 9:11-12)

The power of the Blood of Jesus manifests in magnificent ways! Here are some of the miraculous ways that the power of the Blood of Jesus manifests: *The Blood of Jesus cleanses us from all our sins: sins past, present, and future.* **"...the blood of Jesus Christ his Son cleanseth us from all sin."** (1 John 1:7b)

The Greek definition for the word **"sin"** (ἁμαρτάνω) **hamartanō,** *ham-ar-tan'-o;* prop. to *miss* the mark (and so *not share* in the prize), i.e. (fig.) to *err,* esp. (mor.) to *sin:* for your faults, offend, sin, trespass.[9]

We access the cleansing power of the Blood of Jesus when we acknowledge our sinful ways and ask God for His forgiveness. (1 John 1:9) says: **"If we confess our sins, he is faithful and just to forgive us our sins,**

9 James Strong, *Exhaustive Concordance of The Bible*, Peabody, Massachusetts (1961), pg 10, 264

and to cleanse us from all unrighteousness."

When we sin against God, He will forgive us if we have *truly* repented in our heart for that sinful act against Him. The Blood of Jesus forgave us 2000 years ago, but we must learn how to appropriate the Blood of Jesus in our lives. Don't listen to the lies of the devil saying that God has not forgiven you.

The enemy doesn't want us to receive forgiveness from God, because he wants to continue to torment our minds and cause us to make the same mistakes that God has already forgiven us for our sins.

It is important to note however, that turning away from sin involves confession and repentance before God. God wipes the slate clean and gives us a fresh start; however, we must accept God's forgiveness and move on with our lives! Resist Satan's lies and receive your forgiveness from God so that you will be restored back to your position in fellowship with Christ.

The power of the Blood of Jesus delivers us from danger. I shared my personal testimony about the blood of Jesus in another book that I wrote, "The Power of Giving." This power was demonstrated as I was fasting and taking my prayer walk through my neighborhood.

The Lord directed me to pick up a small stick. As I was walking back to my house, I suddenly saw two pit bull dogs running from the side of a neighbor's house towards me. I said to myself, "This is not my imagination! Two pit bulls are running towards me!" I stretched out the stick towards the dogs and yelled "Jesus!" One of the dogs stopped immediately, but the other dog kept coming towards me. I yelled, "The Blood of Jesus is against you!" In response to these words, I literally saw with my own two eyes that the dog stopped in his tracks and bowed three times.

I then turned around and walked into my house. Shaken, I sat down on my sofa and reflected on what had just happened. The Lord said to me as I sat trembling from shock, "Do you see how much power you have in my Son's name and the power of His Blood?" This was my first time having this kind of encounter, but I saw and experienced the power of the Blood of Jesus, which delivered me from danger.

The Blood of Jesus is a weapon because it is the basis for overcoming the enemy. **"And they overcame him by the blood of the Lamb, and by the word of their testimony; and they loved not their lives unto**

death." (Revelation 12:11)

Jesus is the perfect example of this Scripture because He overcame Satan, his demons, and death, the last enemy, and He did it by the power of His Own Blood and by the power of the Holy Spirit, who raised Jesus from the dead.

The Blood of the Lion of the Tribe of Judah and the Lamb of God overcame Satan and his demons. The Blood of Jesus brought them to defeat and open shame. **"*And* having spoiled principalities and powers, he made a shew of them openly, triumphing over them in it.**" (Colossians 2:15)

The Blood of Jesus is the foundation of cleansing, of deliverance, and for victory against Satan and his demonic forces in heaven and on earth, so call on the Blood of Jesus! It's a powerful weapon that can save your life. Just like it saved mine from the two vicious pit bulls!

A Winner Knows the Power of Forgiveness

THE CRUCIFIXION IS A DEMONSTRATION OF THE LOVE OF GOD FOR HUMANITY AND THE PRICE JESUS PAID FOR OUR SINS. **"For God so loved the world, that he gave his only begotten Son, that whosoever believeth in him should not perish, but have everlasting life."** (John 3:16)

It is the will of God that men and women would spend eternity with Him through Jesus Christ; however, God knows many people have rejected and will reject Jesus and therefore will spend eternity in eternal damnation.

The crucifixion was a brutal, bloody, humiliating, painful and egregious death! John and Matthew give us a glimpse of the crucifixion:

"Then the soldiers of the governor took Jesus into the common hall, and gathered unto him the whole band of soldiers. And they stripped him, and put on him a scarlet robe. And when they had platted a crown of thorns, they put it upon his head, and a reed in his right hand: and they bowed the knee before him, and mocked him, saying, Hail, King of the Jews! And they spit upon him, and took the reed, and smote him on the head. And after that they had mocked him, they took the robe off from him, and put his own raiment on him, and led him away to crucify him." (Matthew 27: 27-31)

Jesus was beaten with a whip and his flesh was exposed to the point where he was not recognized. The suffering of Jesus would be so severe that when He prayed to the Father in the Garden of Gethsemane, he sweated great drops of blood: **"And being in an agony he prayed more earnestly: and his sweat was as it were great drops of blood falling down to the ground."** (Luke 22:44)

In all of Jesus' pain and agony on the cross, he prayed this prayer: **"Then said Jesus, Father, forgive them; for they know not what they do."** (Luke 23:34)

Jesus understood the Power of Forgiveness. He knows Satan is the perpetrator behind all evil and hate. We must follow Jesus' example and forgive others for their wrongdoing towards us and forgive ourselves for the wrongdoing we have done to others.

Jesus paid a very high price for the forgiveness of sins for humanity. The price Jesus paid was with His own blood and His own life! He left the glory of heaven and came down to earth to die for sinful humanity so that we might be forgiven and restored back to our Heavenly Father. Sin requires a death to be taken to receive the gift of forgiveness and righteousness from God. Remember, Scripture says, **"… without shedding of blood, is no remission."** (Hebrews 9:22)

Jesus was the spotless lamb of God; He was the only person who was qualified to die for our sins. He was God in the flesh, yet without sin. In (1 Peter 3:18), the verse reads: **"For Christ also hath once suffered for sins, the just for the unjust, that he might bring** us to God, being put to death in the flesh, but quickened by the Spirit:" The sinless blood of Jesus was required to atone for sinful humanity.

Jesus said when we pray and forgive those who use or hurt us, we are being perfect like our heavenly Father. "Be ye therefore perfect, even as your Father which is in heaven is perfect." (Matthew 5:48)

The Greek definition for the word "perfect" (τέλειος) tĕlĕiŏs, *tel'-i-os;* from *complete* (in various applications of labor, growth, mental and moral character, etc.)[10] It takes maturity to walk in love, and the grace of God to forgive and to pray for those who hurt us.

Forgiveness is so important to God, that Jesus says in (Matthew 6:14-15): "For if ye forgive men their trespasses, your heavenly Father will also forgive you: But if ye forgive not men their trespasses, neither will your Father forgive your trespasses."

God's Word is the final authority and what He says will surely come to pass, so I admonish you to do as the Scriptures say and to pray for your enemies and do good to them that hate you! (Matthew 5:44)

Are struggling to forgive someone in your life, no

10 James Strong, Exhaustive Concordance of The Bible, Peabody, Massachusetts (1961), pg 71,

matter who it is, God requires us to forgive.

Unforgiveness is like a cankerworm or cancer, and it will slowly eat at your flesh, which will eventually make you sick! We are ALL intelligent human beings, and I don't think any of us would willingly agree to allow some pest to constantly eat at our flesh until it deteriorates our physical body unto destruction. Unforgiveness brings destruction, so let it go!

I understand forgiving others who have hurt us can be difficult to the flesh; however, when we agree to forgive as God requires us from His Word, He will give us the grace to do it. He did it for me.

I remember when I was hurt by a person and the Holy Spirit told me to give him a gift. I did not want to give him a gift because I did not feel that I had done anything wrong. Because I wanted to obey God, even though my emotions were speaking contrary to the words of the Holy Spirit, I obeyed. The Holy Spirit gave me specific instructions on what to buy.

When I saw the person, I gave him the gift and there was a sadness that appeared on his face. Once I released the gift, I heard something snap inside of me. The Holy Spirit had broken all emotional ties to this person so the enemy could not use unforgiveness to stop me from receiving the abundance of blessings God has in store for me. Hallelujah!

So, forgiveness is not only about the other person, but it's also about us too. When we hold unforgiveness in our heart, we give the other person power over us. Ouch!

My motto is to make the decision to follow Jesus's example about forgiveness before any offense happens so when I am put in that situation, my emotions will follow the decision to forgive that I have already made. That is to be forearmed against the offense before it comes. Jesus says, **"Woe unto the world because of offences! for it must needs be that offences come; but woe to that man by whom the offence cometh!"** (Matthew 18:7)

In (Ephesians 4:32) the Scripture admonishes us: **"And be ye kind one to another, tenderhearted, forgiving one another, even as God for Christ's sake hath forgiven you."** (Ephesians 4:32)

Final Thoughts to Ponder

GOD LOVES HUMANS. Satan, on the contrary, hates humans and wants to destroy us! Satan is the enemy of God and of the human race. Satan was angry with God, but he couldn't do anything to come against God directly, so his next goal was to destroy human beings, who are made in the Image and Likeness of God.

God wanted Adam and Eve to populate the earth and produce children after His kind. We can see this in (Genesis 1:28a) which says **"And God blessed them, and God said unto them, Be fruitful, and multiply, and replenish the earth, and subdue it…"** It is the will of God for humanity, His creation, to be like him so that we will bring the will of the Father on earth.

Sin interrupted that plan, but God never changed His mind about us and the plans that He has for our lives! The only way for us to be restored back to God's original plan is through Jesus Christ.

In Conclusion

I'VE MENTIONED A FEW POINTS ABOUT EACH OF THE MINDSETS IN THIS BOOK. I encourage you to do a deeper study of each point on your own. God will enlighten you and give you more revelation. We all want to win in life, so we must think like a winner.

The Word of God is the foundation for all ten of these mindsets. If you are serious about changing the way you think, read the Scriptures in this book, and apply them to your life. Your mindset will begin to change. We truly change our lives by changing the way we think.

None of this is possible without a relationship with Jesus Christ. His divine personality is behind the Word of God, so quoting Scripture without the Spirit of God dwelling in you is quoting "the letter" of the law. Scripture warns us in (2 Corinthians 3:6) **"Who also hath made us able ministers of the new testament; not** of the letter, but of the spirit: for the letter killeth, but the spirit giveth life." The Holy Spirit uses these winning mindsets to minister life.

The mindset of a winner will strive to fulfill God's original plan for his or her life as it says in (Ecclesiastes 12:13), "Let us hear the conclusion of the whole matter: Fear God, and keep his commandments: for this is the whole duty of man."

Prayer
of Salvation

IF YOU DON'T KNOW JESUS CHRIST AS YOUR LORD AND SAVIOR, YOU HAVE AN OPPORTUNITY TO RECEIVE HIM INTO YOUR HEART TODAY. All you must to do is to say this prayer out loud:

Lord Jesus, I confess that You are the Son of the living God. I believe in my heart that You died on the cross for my sins and were raised from the dead so that I might have eternal life. I accept you as my Lord and Savior. Thank you, Jesus, for receiving and saving me. In Jesus Name. Amen!

"That if thou shalt confess with thy mouth the Lord Jesus, and shalt believe in thine heart that God hath raised him from the dead, thou shalt be saved." (Romans 10:9)

BIBLIOGRAPHY OF GREEK AND HEBREW REFERENCES

James Strong, *Exhaustive Concordance of The Bible,* Peabody, Massachusetts (1961)

ACKNOWLEDGMENTS

FIRST, I WANT TO ACKNOWLEDGE AND GIVE HONOR TO MY LORD AND SAVIOR JESUS CHRIST. He gave me the vision and empowered me with His ability to write this book. I pray that the words on the pages of this book will bless you, like it did me.

I especially want to thank my family, church family, and friends for praying and supporting me.

I want to thank all the people who encouraged me, prayed for me over the years of my life, you have been a blessing in my life, and I thank God for you.

In addition, I want to thank my editor Lynn C. Jarrett for allowing God to use her creative and editing ability to edit my book. You are a blessing from God, and I thank God for your life. I pray that you will consider starting your own editing company and allow God to use your skills for His Glory!

ABOUT THE AUTHOR

Mary Johnson grew up in the Washington, D.C., Metropolitan area. She is the middle child of seven siblings, of which two are deceased. Mary is an Ordained Minister and has traveled to India, Africa, Panama and in the Washington Metropolitan area to preach the Gospel of Jesus Christ. Mary has a calling on her life to teach the youth the unadulterated Word of God and train them to be disciples for Jesus Christ!

Mary graduated from Bible Faith Global University (BFGU) with a master's degree in Christian Counseling. Mary is the Founder of Building Lives Healing Ministries.

In addition, Mary received a bachelor's degree in Information Systems at Columbia Union College (CUC), in Takoma Park, Maryland. Mary has a passion for Health and Wellness and received her Post Bacca-laureate Certificate from Maryland University of Integrative Health. She has three adorable grandchildren, who bring so much joy to her life. Mary loves sharing the word of God with her grandchildren and teaching them how to pray. Mary is blessed with a wonderful daughter named Stephanie and her husband, Robert. Mary likes to read, cook, and workout.

If you would like to contact Mary, you can reach her at: info@revmaryjohnson.com

INDEX

Made in the USA
Middletown, DE
07 September 2024

59946416R00062